"Not just a book but a valuable tool for readers, coaches and counsellors alike."
— Dr Anthony Llewellyn, Doctor Coach

"Dr. Amy Imms has a brilliant understanding of what burnout feels like in the real world and unfailingly holds your hand as she leads you toward recovery."
— Courtney Sharman, Masters Public Health, mother, TAS

"What a great read! This book not only explains burnout well, it also comes with practical tips that can easily be implemented to help the reader. The section on values was excellent - something we often lose touch with as we get distracted by our daily tasks!"
— **Dr Yumiko Kadota, ex-Plastic Surgery registrar**

"Written with empathy, compassion and understanding, this easy to read guidebook contains practical strategies that inspire hope. I couldn't put it down!"
— **Dr Bambi Ward, medical doctor, PhD creative writing, mother**

"This book is a fantastic resource. I wish I had read it during my internship."
— **Dr Anna Elliston, mother, TAS**

"Burnout, your first 10 steps is just what it says - an accessible, do-able guide that helps stressed people figure out why they feel the way they do, understand that there's hope to feel better, and bring about change to their day-to-day lives and relationships in a lasting way – a must read for self-care!"
— **Rose Jones, Registered Counsellor, VIC**

"A practical and pragmatic approach to tackling a problem we usually are reluctant to acknowledge or address. Thank you from trying to move away from the 'why me/how' to the 'what do I do about it' of burnout."
— **Dr Srishti Dutta**

"As a GP, I see many patients at varying stages of burnout, from people who just don't understand why there's no findable physical cause for their tiredness, to people in the middle of a full-blown breakdown. I feel that burnout is the modern epidemic, born of our increasingly hectic lifestyles, where everything needs to be instant, and technology keeps us switched on at all hours. This book is an easy to read guide to recognising symptoms of burnout and starting to plan the road to recovery. This is a handy reference for those experiencing their own burnout, or for those seeking to aid their friends. As an individual currently juggling busy work hours, a toddler and a sick family member, I don't mind admitting that I can recognise aspects of my own life mirrored in this book, and took away some useful approaches for assessing and planning my time."

— **Dr Sarah Tedjasukmana, GP and mother, NSW**

"In reading this book by Dr Imms I realised the vital difference between simple time off and actual constructive time off. 'How would your life look if you could manage burnout well?' was a game changer for me. Addressing burnout using strategy and activities gave me far better insight, and the values chapter in particular gave me an understanding of my future pathway within medicine.

Looking at the lifestyle I had during those early years of medicine, I realised that life was not meant to just happen in stolen moments. Addressing burnout directly and with purpose has been empowering, and undertaking the steps in this book has been pivotal for recovery."

— **Dr Niki Springett, medical registrar**

Burnout

Your First Ten Steps

Dr Amy Imms

Burnout: Your First Ten Steps

Copyright © Amy Imms 2019 www.dramyimms.com

Illustrations copyright © Amy Imms 2019 www.dramyimms.com

The moral rights of Dr Amy Imms to be identified as the author of this work has been asserted in accordance with the Copyright Act 1968.

First Published in Australia 2019 by Dr Amy Imms.

ISBN

Print ISBN: 978-0-6485710-0-1

E-book ISBN: 978-0-6485710-1-8

All rights reserved. No part of this publication may be reproduced or transmitted by any means, electronic, photocopying or otherwise, without prior written permission of the author.

*Dedicated to Jason,
who has supported me every step of the way.*

*And to Layla, Elsa, Mia, Josie, and Edmund,
for whom I hope for a better future.*

Disclaimer

The content of this book is general in nature, provides no individual clinical advice, and in no way replaces medical consultation. Readers are advised to contact their own doctor or other health professional in relation to any clinical concerns they may have.

Contents

Complementary Workbook vii

Introduction.. 1

Chapter 1 Clarity 5

    Action 1: Are you burnt-out?... 7

    Action 2: Write it all out 10

    Action 3: What are the big issues you are facing?..................... 11

    Action 4: What could your future look like? 12

Chapter 2 Refuel 15

    Action 1: What are your excuses? 16

    Action 2: Clear your diary 18

    Action 3: Schedule fun 19

    Action 4: Relax and reflect.. 20

Chapter 3 See your Doctor 23

    Action 1: Book an appointment... 27

    Action 2: Consider appropriate leave 27

Chapter 4 Compassion 29
   Action 1: Increase awareness 34
   Action 2: How would you treat a friend? 34
   Action 3: Write a self-compassion letter 35
Chapter 5 Boundaries 39
   Action 1: Identifying limits... 40
   Action 2: Respecting your time.. 41
   Action 3: Saying "no".. 42
   Action 4: Boundaries at work.. 44
   Action 5: Separate work and home 46
Chapter 6 Rest 49
   Action 1: Optimise sleep 52
   Action 2: Have a plan...54
   Action 3: Seek medical advice 54
Chapter 7 Think 55
   Action 1: Grounding..58
   Action 2: Mindfulness 59
   Action 3: Gratitude 62
Chapter 8 Connect 65
   Action 1: Join a community or hobby group......................... 69
   Action 2: Reach out and invite..70
Chapter 9 Nourish and Move 75
   Action 1: Regular movement..76

    Action 2: Good nutrition 80
Chapter 10 Values 85
    Action 1: Exploring your purpose 87
    Action 2: Defining your values 89
    Action 3: Journaling 91
    Action 4: Values in your daily life 91
What Next 95
References 99

Complementary Workbook

Overcoming burnout requires taking action, so I've created a workbook that will help you work through the Action exercises in this book. Print it out, and use the chart to keep track of which Actions you have completed. Space is provided in the workbook for you to complete most of the exercises, but some exercises will need a separate journal or notebook so you have plenty of space to write.

Some people find it helpful to repeat selected exercises several months along the journey of recovery, and responses can change significantly in that time. If you wish to do this, simply download another copy of the workbook!

DrAmyImms.com/BurnoutWorkbook

Introduction

When you get to the end of your rope, tie a knot and hang on.
— Franklin D Roosevelt

'Burnout' describes a state of feeling exhausted, overwhelmed, and struggling to cope. It features profound fatigue and depletion, and can have a damaging impact on all aspects of our lives and health: physical, mental, and social[1,2]. Burnout is often experienced when the incessant demands of our workplaces heap-up over a prolonged period of time, and we don't have the resources to meet or reduce those demands[1]. If you are experiencing burnout it often feels like you are just hanging on by a thread, wondering which day you will finally snap; it becomes all-consuming, and the fun parts of life seem to disappear. Often you're strongly aware of the impact this is having not only on your own wellbeing, but on those around you. You feel stuck. You desperately search for a way out, but for every idea you come up with, you can think of ten good reasons why they won't work. Or maybe you're actively hostile towards suggestions or offers of help. You might be beginning to wonder whether there even *is* a way to recover. Well, I'm here to tell you that there is. Recovery takes time and effort, and isn't always easy, but it *is* possible.

Often people wonder if they're an anomaly, part of an exclusive group of people who have somehow found themselves in a mess. It might seem like everyone around you has their lives all worked out, and knows some secret about achieving the perfect work-life balance. The truth is, you are far from alone! According to the Lifeline Stress Poll[3], 77% of Australians experience stress due to work, and 72% experience stress due to finances. In certain professions, burnout affects up to 30-40% of people, and it can affect anyone: employees, business owners, entrepreneurs, parents, carers, students, or volunteers.

Why is burnout such a widespread problem? As with most things, there are several factors at play. Firstly, we have increasing workloads and more expectations placed upon us. Secondly, our time, energy, and finances are often stretched impossibly thin. Thirdly, in a world of stress and busyness, we feel pressure to cope and 'battle on' regardless - because everyone's stressed, right?

Worldwide, there have been climbing rates of mental health issues, as well as a general increase in feelings of discontent. We have poor support resources for those struggling in these areas, and most people end up struggling on their own. Sadly, this leaves many valuable members of our community in compromised life situations, with burnout having been linked to stress-related health problems, car accidents, substance abuse, damaged relationships, and suicide[4]. In the workplace, people suffering from burnout are often less productive, desperate for a break, and sometimes abandon their career altogether. We are left with a devastating situation for individuals, and a tragic loss for the community.

Despite these widespread and escalating challenges, there are ways to overcome burnout. Implementing evidence-based strategies and techniques can help people manage burnout and reduce stress[4], so that they can thrive in their career, maintain strong relationships, and have time and energy for the things they value most.

Burnout Story

When I first met Lisa she was desperate and defeated, with a strong feeling that her problems were too big to solve, and that there was nothing anyone could do. She reluctantly began to identify small things that might help, and we worked through some of the factors that seemed to be affecting her the most, such as how habitually self-critical she had become. Slowly I began to hear a spark of hope filter into our conversations, and some excitement as she relayed to me her stories of progress. Over time she managed to regain her long-lost feelings of contentment with life, and fulfillment from her work.

So, whether you are just starting to see the first signs of burnout, or are at a much more serious stage of burnout, there are things you can do to regain control, contentment, and enjoyment.

Tackling burnout starts with allowing yourself to begin to hope for recovery. Dream of the life you could create: What would your life look like if caring for yourself was a priority? What if you could be more productive? Reduce your stress levels? Have more energy? How would you feel if you had stronger relationships, and found time to do the things you feel most passionate about?

'But I'm too busy', you say. 'I don't have time to read a book', you say. And you leave it for another day, another time... But it doesn't go away, and it doesn't get better. I see people all the time who tell me they put off getting help for years, thinking there was nothing that could help, or because they thought they could solve the problems themselves. But in retrospect, they say they wish they had reached out for assistance much earlier, if only they'd known how much difference it could make.

I know you're busy, and finding time to read a book isn't easy, so I've made this book quick and easy to read. It will take you through ten things you can do to start getting on top of burnout and regaining a life of fulfillment, contentment, and satisfaction. To help you complete the recommended exercises, you can download the accompanying workbook from:

DrAmyImms.com/BurnoutWorkbook

Let's get started!

Chapter 1
Clarity

Till this moment I never knew myself.
— Jane Austen, Pride and Prejudice

If you're like most people, burnout has probably crept up slowly. Stresses gradually mounting, energy levels slowly depleting, but despite this you continue working as hard as ever. You might assume it's 'normal' to feel this way because everyone around you seems to be in the same boat. One day, you suddenly get hit with the realisation that life can't continue this way.

What has made you stop and realise something needs to be done *now*? Perhaps someone has commented on something you have said or done, or on your behaviour, making you stop and reflect; realising there is some truth in their words. Sometimes, it's a consequence of prolonged stress that makes you stop and take notice: a relationship breakdown, a substance addiction, or thoughts of wanting to harm yourself or escape from your life. Whatever it is for you, embrace this realisation, and act for change.

Stop and take a minute to recognise the effect that burnout is having on your life. Is it affecting your work? Relationships? Happiness? Health? Initially, thinking about these things might make you feel flat, and like giving up. But then, knowing that recovery from burnout is possible, allow yourself to imagine your life without burnout. You may remember back to a time when you were content and satisfied in your life. Or, you may dream of a future that you would like to experience. Grasp hold of these possibilities and feelings of hope, and let them drive you forward.

However you came to this point, you know something must change. Often things need to change more than you initially thought, and in ways you hadn't suspected. Before moving forward, it's important to allow yourself to fully acknowledge your current thoughts and emotions. Maybe these emotions have been spilling out for many months, perhaps almost uncontrollably. Or perhaps as challenges have mounted your mind cleverly built walls, suppressed emotions, and consumed your emergency survival resources. When you do finally recognise that you are burnt-out, you may be flooded with a realisation of all the struggles you tried so desperately to push aside. When you acknowledge your emotions, they may pour out. If this occurs, let it happen: this emotional release will help you to move forward. As you experience these emotions, try to keep in mind the hope you have of a more positive future. If any thoughts of self-harm are triggered, you must seek urgent medical attention in order to keep yourself safe. By reading this book, you are taking an active step forward: you have recognised the problem, you are doing something about it, and you are willing to make changes.

Action 1: Are you burnt-out?

Burnout is a term we throw around commonly. But what does it actually mean? How do you know if you are *actually* burnt-out?

Burnout is a term first described by Herbert Freudenberger in 1974, and exactly what it describes has been an issue of ongoing debate[1,2]. It is generally understood to describe a state of being exhausted, overwhelmed, and struggling to cope, often in the context of severe stress and high ideals[1,2]. It happens when there is a mismatch between the resources we have, and what we are trying to do.

So, what does burnout look like for you? Well, maybe you expect a lot of yourself, wanting to do a great job in every area of your life. Maybe you want to be good at your career, as well as trying to be a caring and involved parent, a generous volunteer, a great friend, trying to keep your home respectable, wanting to get fit, and attempting to provide nutritious food for your family. Not only that, you feel like you're expected to do it all with apparent ease and a smile on your face, and even have extra time to relax and do the things you enjoy. Why can't you manage it? It seems like others around you are managing it!?

Perhaps you think if only you can find the right schedule, or get up earlier, it might be achievable. Or maybe you *were* managing to meet your expectations, mostly, until a new overbearing boss arrived, or your mother got sick and required care, or your colleague went on leave and you were expected to take on the extra work, or your child needed extra medical appointments and homework assistance. Whatever your situation is, somewhere along the way, your resources have been pushed beyond their limits.

No matter how strong, intelligent, or resilient you are, you do not have infinite resources of time, energy, or money. The fact that you have reached your limits does *not* reflect personal weakness. It's really important to understand that burnout is not just an individual problem to be addressed by individuals. Burnout is caused by a multitude of factors including workplaces and organisations[1,2], and to address the issues of widespread burnout, these issues must be addressed at an organisational level as well. However, for the moment, focus on yourself and the factors that are more likely to be under your immediate control.

The problem is that it isn't always as easy as you might think to recognise burnout, especially when it's happening to you.

Burnout usually presents with three main elements[1]:

- Exhaustion
- Depersonalisation
- Reduced personal achievement

With burnout, often people will develop these symptoms in the order listed above[5], as opposed to some other illnesses that may present similarly. Initial symptoms tend to be focused around work or the role from which you are feeling burnt-out. For example, you may feel fatigued at the prospect of going to work, but still be energised while socialising or on holiday. However, your ability to recover may reduce over time, with symptoms becoming more persistent.

Below is a list of signs you may notice if you are burnt-out. We all have a different starting point and underlying personalities and tendencies, so the important thing is to identify factors that have *changed* recently. As you read through, keep a tally of how many you identify with.

- Sinking feelings or apprehensiveness before work.
- Use of alcohol to de-stress.
- Feeling unusually emotional or teary.
- Thinking less clearly.
- Doubting your skills and abilities.
- Procrastinating.
- Feeling no joy or interest in work.
- Being less patient than usual.
- Having difficulty sleeping.
- Feeling no hope about life or work.
- Finding decision-making difficult, or second-guessing yourself.
- Turning up to work late, or taking days off for no particular reason.
- Being more irritable, angry, or frustrated than usual.
- Interactions with clients resulting in complaints.
- Making more mistakes than usual.
- Feeling your contribution is unrecognised.

- Feeling exhausted a lot of the time.
- Withdrawing and avoiding socialising.
- Feeling overwhelmed by responsibilities.
- Feeling cynical.
- Loss of empathy.
- A feeling of detachment.
- Feelings of guilt.
- Reduced concentration.
- Feeling unmotivated.
- Doubting your ability to improve your current situation.
- Feeling less efficient than usual.
- Feeling that what you do makes little or no difference.

Out of the items in the list above, how many did you identify with? The more of them you recognise in your life, the more likely it is that you are burnt-out. If you didn't notice many, it may be that you are in the early stages of burnout.

Burnout can be tricky to identify in yourself, so pay close attention if someone else expresses concerns about you or has noticed changes in your behaviour or health.

Action 2: Write it all out

To gain clarity and begin moving forward, it's time to start sorting through your thoughts. I recommend putting pen to paper and writing your thoughts down, rather than just thinking about them. Thinking and worrying about problems uses cognitive effort, so by writing about your thoughts and emotions you free up mental energy to actually work through them. You may also gain new levels of understanding and come up with solutions[6]. You can write your thoughts in or on anything you like, although I would recommend a journal or exercise book so that you can keep everything in one place.

For this exercise, set aside 10-20 minutes when you won't be disturbed. If you can't get undisturbed time, just take any little opportunities you can.

Write down everything that comes to your mind as you consider your current situation, your struggles, your hopes and dreams, or anything else that comes to mind. Think of it like a 'brain dump', or stream of consciousness writing, with no filter between what you think and what you write.

Don't worry if you get stuck after a few minutes and struggle to think of anything else to write, this is normal. Just try to keep on writing, even if you're writing about dinner, the kids, or the view out your window. As you continue, gently try to guide your thoughts back to your present challenges.

Be as honest as you can as you write: do not hold back. No-one else ever has to read it. You can throw it in the bin or burn it once you're done if you want to. Try to break through any stories and partial truths you've been telling in order to survive. Get honest and face your current reality.

Action 3: What are the big issues you are facing?

When you feel depleted and overwhelmed, everything can begin to feel like a confused mess of problems, and it can be quite difficult to know where to start or what to do about them. It's helpful to clearly identify the biggest challenges that are affecting your life at the moment. Aim for a list of only 3-5 core issues. These might be things like: stressful work environment, feeling disconnected, not feeling you're enjoying life, or lacking free time to pursue other interests. If you find yourself wanting to list fifty things and you could keep going, then please do go for it! It may also be helpful to glance back through your 'brain dump' that you did in the previous action, as you may find surprising issues emerge out of stream of consciousness writing.

When you have written down all the issues you are facing, go back and look for common themes. Usually an initial long list ends up being different manifestations of just a handful of core issues. For example, you may have written 'conflict with boss', 'frequently being asked to work overtime', and 'low confidence at work'. You could group these as 'workplace difficulties'. Similarly, 'tension with partner' and 'difficulty connecting with my teenager', might be grouped as 'family relationships'.

This process will guide you towards the key areas which, if you can address them, are likely to provide the biggest improvement in your life.

Action 4: What could your future look like?

Shift your focus from how things are right now, to how you would like things to be; what you hope for. Although it is important to spend time analysing current challenges, don't become too fixated and overwhelmed by your present state. Instead, focus on the future, and write down what you would like your life to look like.

How would your life look if you could recover from burnout? What parts of your life would be eliminated? What new things would be introduced? Aim as high as you like, and dream big.

Take it slow

If you have completed the steps in this chapter, you will hopefully have gained some clarity surrounding what is going on in your life right now. You will have a better idea of how you feel about your current situation, and what the major issues are that need to be addressed or worked though. It can feel overwhelming to see these challenges laid down in writing, but be reassured that they will be addressed slowly. It may have taken you many years to become burnt-out, and will naturally take some time to recover. But the good news is you do not have to solve every one of your problems to significantly improve your situation. Often three to five carefully selected changes can provide huge benefits. The important thing is to keep moving forward at an achievable rate. There is no need to rush through this book in a day, a week, or even a month. You will make the most progress if you can progress slowly enough to make real change along the way.

If you haven't done so already, take time to go through the Actions in this chapter. Don't pressure yourself to complete them in the next 10 minutes, give yourself time to think, and spread it over a few days if necessary. Getting started is the important part for now.

Chapter 2
Refuel

I have come to believe that caring for myself is not self-indulgent. Caring for myself is an act of survival.
— Audre Lorde

You have probably been battling with burnout for a long time, and sacrificing your own health and wellbeing in the process. In this chapter, you will learn how to become better at looking after your health. Here are five very important words: self-care is not selfish!

Although a moderate amount of stress can help you to function better, prolonged severe stress (such as is often experienced in burnout) makes life much more difficult. When you are stressed, your body releases cortisol and adrenaline, and focuses its energy and resources on dealing with perceived threats. In particular, this prolonged stress response affects the three areas of the brain responsible for memory, executive function, and managing emotion[7]. Among other things, this makes it much more challenging for you to make decisions, plan, organise, think flexibly, and cope with complex emotions. All of these brain functions are essential to being able to make the changes you need in order to recover from burnout and to create a more positive career and life for yourself.

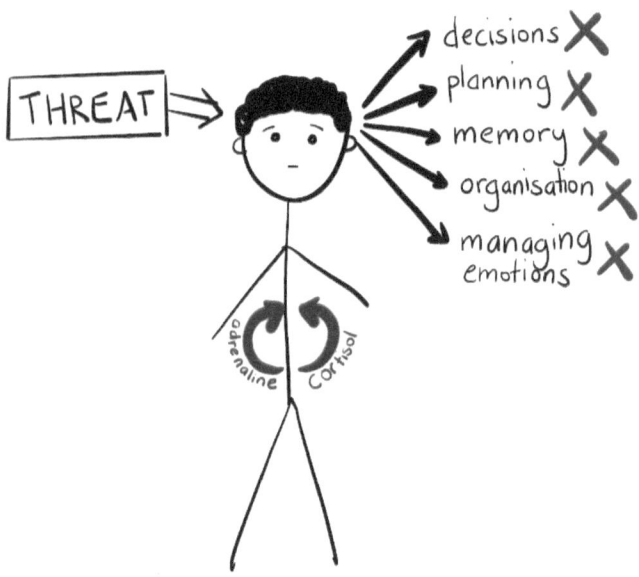

The exercises in this chapter may not solve your problems, but will facilitate some immediate rest and self-care that will put your body and mind in a better state to think clearly and have the energy to focus on longer-term recovery.

Action 1: What are your excuses?
Let's begin by looking at what excuses you use to avoid looking after yourself. This conscious awareness will help you to know exactly what needs to be overcome in order to prioritise self-care.

Grab a journal or piece of paper and list some of the excuses you use to rationalise *not* taking care of yourself. Do you feel guilty when you take time to care for yourself? Do you feel selfish? Do you feel like you should be working, or playing with your kids instead? Do you feel that you're unworthy or undeserving of self-care? Do you feel like you don't have the time or energy for self-care? Or perhaps it's just not something you think about. Write down whatever comes to mind for you.

> **Burnout Story**
> *Anna felt that she had to earn anything good in her life. Simple things like nice food, an evening "off" watching tv, or attending a family birthday party were seen as rewards. If she hadn't worked hard enough, or achieved enough? Those things were denied. The more burnt-out she became, the less she was able to concentrate and be productive, and the more she punished herself by not allowing herself the very things her body and mind so desperately needed to keep going. This vicious cycle of self-denial continued for years. Anna slowly learnt that she was worthy of these things all the time, separate from any achievement, and noticed how much better she was able to function when she nurtured herself in these small ways.*

As you reflect on the list you have written, know that you *are* worthy of self-care. It is not selfish. Taking care of your own health and wellbeing doesn't only help you, but it helps those around you. It leads to better relationships, and it helps us to feel positive about others, allowing us to show more empathy and compassion. The more you take care of yourself, the more you have to give to others.

Consider the main excuses you have been making, and think about what might help you to stop making them. Be alert for your excuses when they crop up in your mind, and swiftly remind yourself that you must prioritise self-care in your life if you want to be healthy and productive.

Action 2: Clear your diary

The next step is to free up some time and reduce busyness, so that you can get the space and rest you need. If you fill every moment of your life with work, family commitments, household tasks, and whatever else seems to fill in the gaps, it becomes impossible to find time to address the issues that have led you to burn out. To create change, you have to be willing to *actually* make changes, which might not always be easy.

Open your diary or look at your calendar and examine the next two weeks. Look for anything at all you could cancel. Be brutal. Right now, *you* need care. And to provide care, you need time. Try not to worry about letting other people down. Most people will be very understanding, and you will find you have a lot more to offer if you take care of yourself. Right now, you need to create as much space as possible for yourself.

Action 3: Schedule fun

Now that you have created some breathing space in your planner, it's time to insert a few things that are going to help you gain some immediate respite and relief.

Take time to deliberately schedule positive activities for the coming weeks. When life gets busy and overwhelming, it's often the enjoyable things that get postponed and neglected, but it is well known that the more that people engage in activities they find pleasant, the better they feel[8,9].

Think about what activities make you feel happy or bring you contentment. They can be anything at all:

- Art or craft.
- Play a video game.
- Read a book.
- Go to the movies.
- Snuggle in front of a fire.
- Go fishing with a friend.
- Play an instrument.
- Have coffee with your Mum or Dad.
- Organise a dinner with friends.
- Go for a swim.
- Play a sport.
- Watch your favourite TV show with dessert.
- Go bushwalking/hiking.
- Do some gardening.
- Go for a bike ride.
- Have a cup of tea.

Schedule at least one of these events each week for the next two weeks. These are now high-priority events in your calendar. Only cancel them in the case of an emergency. When you are doing these enjoyable activities, try to fully immerse yourself in the experience. Do your best to stop thinking about work, family, or your worries. Involve yourself completely in what you are doing right in that moment.

Action 4: Relax and reflect

Look at the free time you have remaining in your calendar in the next few weeks, and schedule in some blocks of time purely for relaxation or reflection, such as:

- Physical activity.
- Meditation.
- Walking in nature.
- A bath, or simply lying down, with your favourite music playing.
- Getting a massage.
- Reading through this book or doing some of the exercises.

These activities differ from the enjoyable activities you scheduled in the last exercise by being specifically about personal relaxation, or creating time and space to think and reflect. Group activities, for example, would be less conducive, and likewise high-thought or complex activities such as a sport or playing an instrument, are not going to create opportunities to think or relax.

Schedule at least two of these events each week for the next two weeks. This may sound hard, and your brain may already be coming up with reasons why you can't possibly find the time, but remind yourself that it is important. Just like the fun items you scheduled, these are now high-priority events in your calendar, to be cancelled only for emergencies. If you don't have time set aside to work through burnout, it isn't going to happen. Perhaps for a short while you'll make some progress, but it won't be long before you feel overwhelmed again, and for busyness, stress, and fatigue to crowd in and thwart your plans.

Make time. Here are the first three steps in summary:
- Simplify by clearing your diary of all non-essential activities for the next two weeks.

- Schedule one fun activity each week for the next two weeks.
- Schedule two relaxing or reflective activities each week for the next two weeks.

At this point you have only made changes for the next two weeks. At the end of the first week, reflect on how you went. Did you manage to stick to your schedule? Were your plans realistic? Do you want to increase the time you spend on fun or relaxing activities? With these thoughts in mind, continue to apply the three changes listed above to your schedule, making sure to do so ahead of time. How frequently you do this will depend on how your life is structured - some of you may be able to alter your schedule easily for the upcoming week, whereas others will need to make changes several weeks in advance.

Chapter 3
See your Doctor

Early diagnosis is so important because the earlier a mental illness can be detected, diagnosed and treatment can begin, the better off that person can be for the rest of his or her life.

— Rosalynn Carter

Before progressing further, it's important to find out whether you have any other physical or mental illnesses that may be contributing to your current state. Every medical journey should begin with a visit to your GP. They are your guide, it's their job to make sure your path to good health is safe and is pointing in the right direction.

> **Burnout Story**
> *Geoff had felt burnt-out for many years, but he didn't tell anyone because he felt like a failure. He barely wanted to admit it to himself, let alone his colleagues, or even worse: his boss. He relied upon*

his job to support his family, and he'd worked so hard to get there. He felt that he needed to maintain the appearance of being strong, and capable of handling everything that came his way. He was so afraid of anyone else finding out, and so embarrassed by his 'failure', that it took five years to see his GP about it. His GP was able to help him work through his struggles and get the support he needed, and he was even able to make some positive changes in the workplace. He eventually told his close friends and family about it, and his fears about their reactions didn't eventuate. They were supportive and became an important part of his recovery. He wished he had talked to people and seen someone about it right back at the beginning, instead of hiding in shame and embarrassment.

There are two things to consider:

1. Firstly, it's possible you may *not* be burnt-out at all. There is no test that will flawlessly diagnose burnout, and it has many symptoms that overlap with other illnesses[10]. It is vital to get the diagnosis correct early on, so that you can receive appropriate treatment.
2. Secondly, if you are experiencing burnout it is possible that you may also have other illnesses that are contributing to, or exacerbating, your symptoms. In order to make significant progress towards overcoming burnout, these extra issues require appropriate treatment and must not be ignored.

There are many physical illnesses that can cause both psychological symptoms and fatigue. Illnesses such as heart conditions, thyroid dysfunction, bowel disorders, vitamin and mineral deficiencies, and even cancer[11] can cause these symptoms. For example, if you have an iron deficiency then no amount of burnout management is going to completely resolve your fatigue. For this reason, don't assume that burnout is the only possible cause for your symptoms, as this may delay diagnosis and treatment of other serious illnesses. Anyone who thinks they are burnt-out must see their GP or family doctor to rule out other diagnoses. This is particularly important if you have noticed any new or worsening symptoms.

Burnout Story

Elise felt overworked, exhausted, and burnt-out. She made several attempts to improve things both personally and at work. She managed to cut back on her overtime, she started going for evening walks, and tried some meditation exercises. But she felt tired all the time, and nothing seemed to be making any significant difference. After a few months, she finally built up the courage to see her GP, not really expecting her doctor to be able to help much. To her surprise, the routine tests her doctor did showed that she was very iron deficient! After treating her iron deficiency, her energy levels returned almost to normal. Once she knew her physical health was in good shape, she reassessed her previous feelings of overwork and burnout, and realised that although she hadn't actually been burnt-out, the changes she had made had

> *really helped her enjoy work more. Her GP encouraged her to continue these things, pointing out that they could help to prevent future burnout, but to return for another review if any of her symptoms returned.*

As well as burnout having overlap with certain physical illnesses, it's important to know that many symptoms of burnout also overlap with mental illnesses such as anxiety and depression[10]. For this reason, it is again important to see your GP for correct diagnosis. If you *are* suffering from burnout, it is possible that in addition to burnout you may also have coexisting issues or mental illnesses such as substance abuse, bipolar disorder, an eating disorder, or obsessive-compulsive disorder. Treatment for burnout, when in conjunction with complex issues such as these, can be more difficult, and you will need to make a plan with your GP in relation to management and recovery. If you would like to have some insight into your personal situation before visiting your GP, you can do a self-assessment[12] for depression, anxiety, and bipolar disorder at blackdoginstitute.org.au. Self-assessments won't necessarily give you an accurate diagnosis, but may give you an indication to begin with. If you think you may be experiencing symptoms of an illness other than burnout, please do not proceed with the advice in this book. See your doctor, wait until your illness is well managed, and then if burnout is still present, proceed with the advice in this book only if your doctor or other therapist feels that is appropriate for you. As mentioned previously, correct diagnosis is important for proper treatment and positive outcomes.

Action 1: Book an appointment

If you haven't had your current symptoms fully checked out by a doctor, or if your symptoms have changed since your last check-up, please book in now for an assessment. Most people with suspected burnout will have several issues to discuss, which will likely be addressed over a number of appointments.

Action 2: Consider appropriate leave

Now is a good time to consider whether burnout is affecting you enough that a period of leave would be beneficial. In some cases it's more helpful to continue working while addressing burnout, as taking too much time off work can lead to increasing apprehension about returning to your role, or it can fuel escapism as an unhelpful coping strategy. For others, leave from work can be an important part of the recovery process. Have a chat to your doctor, and together you will be able to make a decision about what is best for your situation. If you do take leave, make sure that you have a plan for how you will use it so that you can optimise the benefits it can provide toward recovery.

Chapter 4
Compassion

If your compassion does not include yourself it is incomplete.
— Jack Kornfield

Over the last three chapters, you have spent considerable time and effort focusing on your own health, and deliberately creating opportunities for self-care. How does this make you feel? Has it come easily, or has it made you feel uncomfortable? Perhaps you have been reading through this book and nodding along, but found that there is something stopping you actually taking action. Think back over your adult life, and reflect on whether you have generally found it difficult to take care of yourself. If so, you are not alone.

From early childhood, we are taught a lot about how to take care of our bodies, but very little about how to take care of our minds. We are taught the importance of eating well, exercising, and brushing our teeth, but we are not taught how to manage our mental health in busy or stressful times. We are even taught the importance of kindness and care towards others, but almost nothing about how or why we should be kind to ourselves. Most people are highly self-critical and judgemental toward themselves, with a harsh inner monologue keeping self-criticisms at the forefront of our minds. If we don't learn to be kind and compassionate toward ourselves, we struggle to prioritise our own wellbeing, which can not only create the perfect recipe for burnout but also be an enormous barrier to recovery.

When we try to find solutions to our struggles, and implement new strategies, they are inevitably imperfect. Although we may experience a level of improvement, we end up frustrated and feeling that we have failed at yet another attempt to recover[13]. Instead, accepting our struggles, showing self-compassion, and facing the fact that we will inevitably have issues in our lives, actually ends up doing far more good for our wellbeing. Self-compassion is about increasing our capacity to accept, rather than resisting what comes our way[13]. So if you make a mistake, or fail at something, or come up against a roadblock along your journey to recovery, don't lose heart. Be kind and compassionate to yourself. You can always reassess the situation, try something different, or work towards an alternative outcome.

When we have challenges in our lives, there is more at play than simply our own conscious reactions and emotions. We often think that if we can find the right approach, we can be perfectly healthy, and overcome any psychological challenges we face. The reality is that a significant component of our physical and mental health is dictated by our genes and our early life environment and circumstances. You can certainly improve your experience of your life through conscious effort and the application of certain techniques, but part of that process is accepting you may have ongoing struggles, and having compassion for yourself throughout these experiences.

Having said this, self-compassion doesn't mean accepting what is happening to you and doing nothing about it, but rather it is about accepting yourself as you experience struggles or pain[15]. If you can develop self-compassion, you will have a powerful tool to use throughout life as you face challenges. Self-compassion is a protective mechanism that can reduce depression and anxiety, and negative emotions such as fear, irritability, hostility, and distress[14]. Self-compassion can be particularly helpful when our bodies are under stress. Stress can arise from many sources: internal, external, physical, mental, or emotional. Whatever the catalyst, stress triggers a complex response from our neurological and endocrine systems, such as the release of cortisol and adrenaline[15]. This hormone release results in symptoms including increased heart rate, rapid breathing, muscle tension, and sweating[15]. In contrast, self-compassion triggers feelings of warmth and safety, which deactivates our stress response, and promotes the release of the hormone oxytocin instead, leading to positive emotions and feelings of connection and attachment.

Self-compassion is not passive or self-indulgent. It is an active process stemming from the theory that all humans are deserving of compassion. It is not something that is earned. We need to show compassion towards ourselves even when we feel like we don't deserve it; when we have made a mistake or feel that a particular undesirable situation is our fault. Any and all human suffering, regardless of cause, deserves a kind and compassionate response. Dr Kristin Neff is one of the world's leading experts in the science of self-compassion, and this is how she describes its three key elements[14]:

1. **Self-kindness versus self-judgement.** We must be kind and gentle with ourselves when we face suffering, whether it be through failure, imperfection, or challenges outside of our control. It is helpful to accept these challenges as a normal part of the human experience, rather than fighting against them and becoming angry, frustrated, or self-judgemental.
2. **Common humanity versus isolation.** Often when we are suffering we feel isolated. It is helpful to recognise that all humans suffer and are imperfect. Through suffering, we are participating in a shared human experience.
3. **Mindfulness versus over-identification.** The aim is to experience your emotions without either suppressing them or exaggerating them. We recognise our suffering as part of the bigger picture, and observe our emotions

with mindful awareness, just as they are. This helps us to not get swept up in unhelpful cycles of negative reactivity.

Although self-compassion might initially appear simple, many people have significant difficulty actually applying the concept to their own thought processes, which is hardly surprising considering how many years of ingrained thought patterns they are trying to change.

Burnout Story

Ellyn found understanding the interplay of genes, environment, and circumstances life-changing. She had spent her whole life trying to "fix" all her struggles, and thought that if she could only find the "right approach," or apply strategies "properly," then all would be well. But she came to realise that there were parts about herself that would not change easily, or even at all. And that these parts of her were part of what made her unique, and not a problem to be overcome. Rather than finding these more fixed aspects of genetics and past circumstances restrictive, she found them liberating. She was able to give herself permission to use all the resources available to her to create the best life possible, without striving for an end-goal of perfection. She has gone from being lost, frustrated, and defeated, to loving her life and being content with her choices.

Action 1: Increase awareness

Over the next few days, carry a journal or notebook with you and, paying attention to your reactions to personal suffering, jot down anything you notice. Be particularly on the lookout for moments when you are suffering. This could be because you make mistakes, don't meet your own expectations, loneliness, embarrassment, grief, pain, exhaustion, and so on. In these situations, try to capture the exact words and phrases you tell yourself. Write them down, and after several days read back through them and see if there are any common themes or trends. Do the things you tell yourself surprise you? How do you feel about the way you speak to yourself?

Action 2: How would you treat a friend?

Use your journal again for this exercise designed by Dr Kristin Neff and Chris Germer[16]. The first step is to think about a time when a good friend felt bad about themselves or was going through a challenging time. Write down the things you would tend to do or say in this sort of situation, and what tone of voice you would use.

Secondly, think of a time *you* have struggled or felt bad about yourself. How do you usually respond to yourself? What words do you use in these situations? What tone of voice do you use? What actions do you take?

Reflect on the differences between these responses. Why do you think they exist? Why do you treat yourself differently to how you treat others?

The final step is to consider what might happen if you responded to yourself in the same way you respond to friends. Write down some thoughts about how this might change the way you feel during difficult times.

> **Burnout Story**
> *Alex found the concept of treating himself in the same way that he would treat a friend a foreign concept. Intellectually it made sense to him - he understood that he was just as deserving of that compassion than anyone else. But to emotionally reconcile that with how he had unconsciously treated himself his entire life was extremely challenging. He genuinely felt that every self-critical thought he had was a reflection of fact, not opinion.*

Action 3: Write a self-compassion letter [16]

Begin by thinking of something that makes you feel inadequate or bad about yourself. This could relate to any aspect of your life: your body, work, relationships, habits, skills, or anything else. Write down the emotions you feel as you think about this.

Then, imagine you have a friend who is unconditionally loving, accepting, kind, and compassionate. Imagine that this friend can see your strengths, but also your weaknesses, and doesn't judge you for them. Think about how this friend might feel toward you, accepting you just as you are. This friend knows that you are only human, they are forgiving of your mistakes, and they understand your life experiences.

Write a letter to yourself from the perspective of this imagined friend. What would this friend say about the thing you wrote about at the beginning of this exercise? How would they convey their compassion to you, especially about the pain you feel when you judge yourself? What would this friend write in order to remind you that you are only human, and that all people have strengths and weaknesses? Infuse your letter with this friend's acceptance, kindness and care.

Here is an example of what your letter could look like:

> *To my friend,*
>
> *I see how much you care about your work, and how much time and effort you put into helping those in your care. I know you blame yourself when outcomes aren't what you'd like them to be. I know how meticulously you look for any mistakes you've made, or anywhere you could have done better, but no matter how perfectly you do your job, or how hard you work, you can't control everything. As unfortunate as it is, some bad outcomes are inevitable. You need to remember that you're only human. Everyone makes mistakes, everyone is imperfect. You cannot be perfect, and you're the only one that expects you to be.*
>
> *I know it's not easy to change the way you feel about these things, and I know you will always*

care deeply about those around you. But you have to do something. Don't stay up at night worrying. Go out with your friends! Use us as a mirror to look at yourself differently, with love. You are more than your career, or the mistakes you've made.

Sometimes I worry you're unable to see the amazing person you are. I see your kind heart. I see your compassion and empathy. Your creativity and musical talent. Your infectious smiles. Your magical ability to whip up a gourmet meal in minutes. These are the parts of you that I want you to know are there, every day.
From,
Your Loving Friend

Your letter may be very different to this example, depending on what issues or aspects of yourself you choose to write about. There's no right or wrong way to write your letter: it may be longer, shorter, or a completely different style.

Set the letter aside for a while, then go back and read through it again. Let yourself feel the compassion it provides.

Summary

After doing these exercises, you will become more aware of when you're being self-critical and when you're showing yourself kindness. When you notice self-criticism, think back to what you wrote in these exercises, and see if you can respond kindly. You may even like to carry a little self-compassion letter with you, or memorise a short phrase, such as:

> *I know this self-critical part of me is trying to protect me in some way, but it isn't helpful. I acknowledge the suffering I feel in this moment, and I choose to respond with kindness and compassion.*

Through this conscious effort to change your internal monologue, you will reduce your stress response to self-criticism and increase positive and compassionate thoughts.

Don't be discouraged if the exercises in this chapter feel challenging. Remember that you may have spent your whole life being self-critical, and shifting your internal thoughts will require practice, and perhaps even some guidance from a professional.

Chapter 5
Boundaries

Insanity is doing the same thing over and over again, but expecting different results.

— Rita Mae Brown

If you want to recover from burnout, something in your life must change. The way forward must be different, in some way, from what led you to this point. The boundaries we set in our lives strongly influence the way we relate to our environment and other people, and help us to navigate our lives. Examining and altering these boundaries can be helpful for many people.

Setting strong boundaries can improve your relationships, and also help you manage your schedule, ensuring that you do not overfill it. Leaving space in your schedule enables you to make time for self-care, fun, relaxation, and the things you value most in life. It is important not to feel guilted into overbooking your time, or feel pressured by other people's expectations. If you have boundaries, stick to them. You may be trying to juggle a whole variety of commitments, all competing for your time and energy, such as work, family, social commitments, and community engagements[17]. This can lead to symptoms such as anxiety, irritability, stress, poor appetite, fatigue, reduced life satisfaction, poor relationships, and may make you feel the desire to quit your job[18].

Setting boundaries can be difficult, and as mentioned earlier, can often make people feel guilty. But you must try to avoid feeling guilt for maintaining your boundaries. Knowing your limits and boundaries—and sticking to them—is vital for your own well-being. It's also important so that you have energy to give to others. If you feel guilty for saying 'no', remind yourself that saying 'no' now will allow you the time and space you need to recover from burnout, and then you might be able to say 'yes' more often later.

Action 1: Identifying limits

Your boundaries will be unique to you, and it's ok for your boundaries to be vastly different from others'[18]. Pay attention to your limits, and learn to recognise when they are being over-stepped. You need to decide what is appropriate for you, and what isn't, in terms of your relationships and life[19]. You may have some boundaries which are absolute, and others that you intuitively modify depending on circumstance[19]. For example, you may have an absolute boundary that you never tolerate sexist remarks, and this boundary exists in all contexts. However, you may have a rule that you do not take work home with you, but you're comfortable shifting this boundary under certain circumstances, like when you could really use a trusted sympathetic ear, or need someone to help you validate how you reacted to a situation at work. When you feel uncomfortable or stressed, stop to check whether a boundary has been crossed or pushed. Sometimes it isn't until boundaries are actually broken that we realise they existed in the first place. If you find yourself feeling resentment towards someone, consider whether that person has been repeatedly overstepping your boundaries.

Make a list of your boundaries, adding as much detail as you can to each one. Make note of how firm or variable you think each one is. Use this list to help guide your actions and decisions. Seeing your boundaries written down may help you to identify which, if any, are currently being overstepped. This will help you recognise areas of your life that may need to be addressed, or areas where boundaries need to be established or strengthened. Revisit your list of boundaries at a later date, and see if you have been able to make progress towards living more in line with them. Remember also, that boundaries don't necessarily stay the same forever - your personal limits can change over time.

Action 2: Respecting your time

Put some boundaries around how you spend your time. This will help you to prioritise the things that are important to you, and give you the space and time you need in order to recover from burnout. Boundaries about how you spend your time can help you to maintain a healthy work-life balance, keep you from over-booking your schedule, and also make it easier to set aside uninterrupted periods of time dedicated to specific activities, such as 'Saturday morning family time', or 'running with a friend on Monday evenings', or 'Tuesday lunchtime, working through some of the material in this book'.

Now is a good time to check in to see how you are going with making the changes to your schedule we covered in Chapter 2. Have you managed to keep your schedule simplified? Or have more little events and commitments edged their way in? Are you prioritising your fun and relaxation times, or are they disappearing all too easily as new things crop up?

Once a week, find a time when you can easily spend two minutes glancing through the week ahead, perhaps after breakfast on a Sunday morning, or during your Friday lunch break: whatever works consistently for you. In this time, follow the steps you completed in Chapter 2:

1. Simplify and cancel all non-essential events.
2. Schedule one fun activity for the week.
3. Schedule at least two times for relaxation or reflection.

It may be helpful to set a recurring reminder on your phone to prompt you to do this.

Action 3: Saying "no"

Saying "no" is an essential skill for maintaining your boundaries. When someone approaches you with a request for a favour, do you have trouble saying "no"? Do you inwardly groan, and let slip a "yes, of course!" before you can stop yourself? You probably spend the next three days figuring out how you can get out of it, because you already have too much on your plate. Or if someone goes to hug you, and you don't feel comfortable, are you able to say "no" or find another way to maintain this boundary? If you can learn to say "no", it will be an extremely useful tool for you as you recover from burnout.

The question is, how do you say "no" without offending people or feeling rude?

If someone asks you to do something, try buying yourself time by saying:

- "Thanks so much for the opportunity. I'll think about whether that's something I can commit to and get back to you", or
- "That sounds wonderful, thanks for inviting/asking me! Let me check my diary and I'll get back to you tomorrow".

This allows you to engage and make the other person feel heard, but avoids having to give them an immediate response. You can then take your time to consider your wisest response, given your finite resources of time and energy.

Some situations, such as an unwanted hug, are obviously not suitable for this kind of delayed response. In this case, you need a firm decision and swift response, right then in the moment. Take note of these things when they arise, and think through where your boundaries sit in that area. Try to think about any changes in the boundary under different likely circumstances. This will help you to have a predefined clear boundary in mind, rather than trying to make a rapid confused decision in the moment. You then need to have the courage to stick to it, and explicitly and clearly state it when necessary. You might like to have a brief phrase you can use when it arises. If you decide that you won't accept hugs from clients, you may decide that your general response will be to offer your hand instead, and say "I have no hugging rule at work, sorry!".

Don't over-explain yourself when you strengthen a boundary or say "no". You are allowed to set your boundaries, and make your own decision, for your own reasons. Explaining your reasons too much can result in the other person questioning your explanation or trying to talk you out of your decision. You could say something like "I'm flattered that you asked me to do this! I can't commit to taking this on at the moment, but I'd love to make a donation or help share the word about your event". There are plenty of ways you can show your support for something, through encouragement or small actions, without taking on the specific task someone has requested.

You will become more comfortable using these strategies the more you practice them, and through experimentation you will find the approach that feels best for you. Respect your time and personal space, and keep your boundaries firm. If it is appropriate, make sure you clearly communicate your boundaries, so that other people know what to expect from you. People will inevitably test and push your boundaries, but through your behaviours and actions you can keep them firm.

Action 4: Boundaries at work
In order to address burnout, it's important to think further about your work, or other role that is making you burnt-out, and

whether there are boundaries you can strengthen. These may relate to things like:

- How many hours you work.
- Whether you work overtime, or how much, or under what circumstances.
- Who you give out your phone number to.
- Whether you are comfortable accepting hugs from colleagues, or from clients.
- Who you are comfortable adding to your personal social media networks.

Sometimes it may seem impossible to create the boundaries you desire because of your workplace structure or culture. But if you can approach people with a reasoned argument that highlights the benefits of the change for the workplace or yourself personally, you may be pleasantly surprised.

The issues you face at work do not only affect your work life, but also filter through to the rest of life. To set boundaries, it's helpful to consider what you value in life, and then look at your boundaries in relation to these things. For example, if you're passionate about writing a novel, you may set strict work hours so that you actually have time to write. Or if you enjoy playing a sport, you may strictly work no overtime on Wednesdays to allow you to attend each game. Or if you want to spend more time with your family and friends then you may make a rule that you never do anything relating to your work on weekends or evenings.

Write down all the boundaries you identify that relate to your work. Once you have your list, brainstorm some ideas that might help you to establish, strengthen, or maintain these boundaries.

Burnout Story

Denise felt flustered and anxious at work, largely because she was frequently interrupted by other staff who needed her to address issues, answer questions, take calls, and complete tasks. Because of this, she found it difficult to concentrate, and sometimes found herself making mistakes because interruptions disrupted her workflow and she would forget things. She was able to come up with some strict, practical boundaries that enabled the issues to be addressed in a timely and efficient manner that minimised unexpected interruptions. Her work was much more enjoyable when she could fully concentrate on and complete it without worrying about being interrupted. She made fewer mistakes, and felt less anxious as her days felt more structured and predictable.

Action 5: Separate work and home

One of the biggest challenges is when work issues take hold and end up dominating our whole lives. This is particularly difficult for people who are self-employed or work from home. Work can overtake your life physically, for example by receiving work communication out of hours, or taking work home to complete, or it may manifest as a mental pressure if you struggle to 'switch off'. This often results in people having trouble truly relaxing or engaging in other areas of their lives because their minds continue to dwell on work issues. If this is the case for you, it means that your mind is not getting enough down-time to recover.

It is important to set strict boundaries between 'work time' and 'non-work time'. Firstly, avoid any work-related communication outside of official work hours. You may be able to set up strategies for yourself such as not checking work emails outside of work hours, or not talking to colleagues about work if you see them socially. If the line between your work and home life is becoming blurred, you may even need to have a conversation with colleagues or your boss about the issues affecting you. For example, it may be necessary to request not to be contacted after-hours, and instead suggest that whoever is trying to contact you could set up a meeting for the following workday. These sorts of measures will help give your mind rest when it's needed. Further strategies to achieve this mental rest will be explored in Chapter 7.

If your boundaries have been neglected and require a lot of work to restore, then take things slowly. Start off with the issue you feel is affecting you most, and begin by implementing one or two actions that will make the most positive change.

Chapter 6
Rest

Learn from yesterday, live for today, look to tomorrow, rest this afternoon.

— Charles M Schulz

Fatigue is often a big feature of burnout, so getting adequate sleep is very important. Sleep is an underestimated element in terms of its impact on our health. We all know that if we don't get enough sleep we feel tired the next day, but lack of sleep can have far greater effects than just tiredness. Prolonged poor sleep can cause a whole range of issues: poor concentration, problems with memory, low attention levels, feelings of sadness, and irritability[20]. All these things can have a big impact on how we perform at work, also affecting our motivation levels in general, as well as our home lives, such as our patience with our children.

It takes significant emotional energy to address burnout. Therefore, everything you can do to reduce fatigue and increase energy levels will help. When you are burnt-out, fatigue and sleep difficulties can arise for various reasons, such as insufficient rest created by poor boundaries, or fatigue due to emotional stress. Perhaps you have been working extra hours to compensate for what you perceive as reduced performance due to burnout. Perhaps sleep is eluding you because you are anxious or worried about something.

You may have even developed destructive patterns to deal with poor sleep, without realising it. You might be relying on stimulants such as coffee, energy drinks, and cigarettes to get you through your day, or perhaps relying on alcohol or sleeping tablets to switch your mind off at night. These coping strategies are common, but unhelpful in the long term, and need to be addressed as early as possible. You may want to book an appointment to see your doctor if you feel that you are becoming dependent on these sorts of strategies.

Burnout Story

James was struggling with issues at work and home: he had a stressful project at work, his boss expected him to work extra hours at the drop of a hat, his toddler wasn't sleeping well, and he felt like he and his wife were constantly arguing. But the biggest thing that he felt affected him day to day was his sleep. If he could just sleep better, he felt that he'd be able to manage everything else better, and find a way forward. He was drinking a few glasses of wine at night to help him fall asleep, but soon enough he'd be wide awake again. It felt like hours passed as he thought back over the stresses of the previous day, before finally dozing... only to be woken by his alarm clock. After seeing his doctor, he put all the energy he could muster into trying to improve his sleep. He cut out the alcohol altogether, he started going for an evening run (which he'd always enjoyed in the past), and he used some relaxation exercises to help get back to sleep when he awoke during the night. It felt like hard work, and he nearly gave up a few times, but after a week, he noticed some improvements. A few weeks later, his sleep was vastly improved. He was so relieved to emerge from his foggy sleep deprivation, and felt able to begin tackling the other challenges in his life.

Action 1: Optimise sleep

There are many simple things[21] you can do to optimise your chances of getting restorative sleep.

Give these strategies a try:

1. **Your bed is for sleep**. Only use your bed for sleeping and intimacy. Avoid doing any other activities in bed, such as watching television or checking social media. This will help to strengthen the mental association between your bed and sleep.
2. **Consistency**. Be as consistent as you can with your sleep and wake times, on both weekdays and weekends. It can also help to be consistent with the timing of other daily routines such as social interactions and mealtimes[22].
3. **Preparation ritual**. Prepare your body and mind for sleep by creating a short ritual, helping to signal that sleep is approaching. This could be a hot drink, reading a book, or simply a predictable sequence of bedtime preparations such as brushing your teeth, saying goodnight to your kids, having a glass of water, turning the light off and getting into bed.
4. **Screens off**. If you struggle to fall asleep at night, try avoiding all screens for one hour before bed. If you really must use your phone, experiment with a screen colour that is less disruptive to sleep, or use the nighttime mode. Avoiding bright lights at night-time aids the function of your circadian rhythm, which is your natural sleep-wake cycle. To help your circadian rhythm, it can also be helpful to open curtains and

have sunlight coming into your room first thing in the morning.

5. **Relaxation**. To help your mind switch off, try relaxation exercises either before or in bed, such as progressive muscle relaxation, breathing exercises, imagery, or meditation.
6. **Avoid naps**. Daytime naps are best avoided, as they disrupt your ability to fall asleep at night. Instead, try to push yourself to stay up until close to your normal bedtime.
7. **Light meals**. Try having a light evening meal several hours before bedtime. Some people have difficulty falling asleep if they have heavy meals too close to bedtime, so experimenting with the size and composition of your evening meal may help, particularly if you suffer from reflux when lying down in bed.
8. **Exercise early**. Exercising in the afternoon or early evening can help with sleep, but be aware that physical activity too close to bedtime can disrupt sleep by making you more alert. Aim to have at least a couple of hours between exercising and going to bed.
9. **Limit drugs**. Caffeine, alcohol and cigarettes all interfere with sleep, and should be avoided late in the day.

Some of these strategies can affect your ability to fall asleep, but others affect the *quality* of your sleep. Sleep quality is not as easily noticed, so rather than simply concentrating on how long it took you to fall asleep, or how many hours you slept for, it's helpful to pay attention to how refreshed you feel the next day.

Action 2: Have a plan

It's helpful to have a plan for what you will do if you have difficulty sleeping. If you spend more than 20 minutes trying to get to sleep, it's best to get up for a while to avoid becoming frustrated, which will contribute to your sleeplessness. It's a vicious cycle. Instead, get up and leave the bedroom. Remember your bedroom is *only* for sleep and intimacy. Keep the lights dim, choose a quiet activity, such as drawing or reading, and then try again.

Action 3: Seek medical advice

It's important to note that there are many medical conditions that can cause or contribute to sleep difficulties and feelings of fatigue, so if symptoms persist, you should see your doctor to consider causes other than burnout. There are also several other strategies that can improve sleep, which are not mentioned above but that may be appropriate for you to try. So again, if sleep difficulties persist, seek advice from your health professional.

Chapter 7
Think

Happiness lies not in finding what is missing, but in finding what is present.

— Tara Brach

Our minds spend most of the day chattering away about our lives, the past, the future, people, work, and ourselves. Our ability to analyse the past and imagine the future is critical to success in life and work. This skill helps us to solve problems, come up with new ideas, respond to complex situations, and be creative. However, our brains use these very same abilities in ways that are counterproductive. Our minds are so good at thinking about the past and future, that it can be incredibly difficult to focus on the present for long at all. As burnout progresses, you may find that you develop even more ingrained patterns of worrying about the future and dwelling upon the past. When people spend more of their time being present, they can cope better with challenges, experience enhanced concentration, feel less stressed, process emotions more easily, and experience more joy[23,24].

If you are struggling to concentrate on the present, the good news is there are things you can do to keep your mind in the present more often. They're not hard to implement, however they will take some practice. At first, structured exercises such as mindfulness can feel a little awkward, uncomfortable, or frustrating. But they do get easier, and over time will feel more natural.

Throughout our lives there will be challenges, sadness, grief, and many other difficulties that are part of the normal and full human existence. And there are other times when being present is painful. Mentally escaping the present is a protective survival mechanism in some circumstances, such as if you are suffering from post-traumatic stress disorder. If you have post-traumatic stress disorder, or think being present might be traumatic for you, then please do not attempt mindfulness or meditative exercises, such as those in this chapter, without the supervision of an appropriate trained health professional. Most people will experience some minor initial discomfort when learning to focus on the present, but if your discomfort is excessive or prolonged, please stop until you have sought professional advice.

Spending more time with our minds focused on the present helps us to reduce our negative thought pathways, but this is only one part of the solution. We can also deliberately increase our positive thought pathways. Each time you repeat a thought process, then that neural pathway grows stronger, and it is then easier for your brain to re-enter that particular thought process at other times. So, as we learn to be 'present' more, the negative thought pathways decrease in strength. Similarly, when we repeatedly foster times in which our brain enters a positive thought pattern, that pathway becomes stronger and stronger. The stronger thought pathways are those that our brain more automatically 'defaults' into. This can be achieved through exercises such as focusing on things you're grateful for, participating in activities you find enjoyable, being creative, spending time in nature, being physically active, or engaging in positive relationships.

The remainder of this chapter will teach you a range of strategies to assist with stress, be more present, and increase positive thoughts and emotions. Try to learn them all, and imagine that you're filling your tool-kit with strategies that you can then choose from depending on the situation.

Action 1: Grounding

During your life you will inevitably find yourself in situations where you get caught up in negative thought patterns, feeling anxious, or demoralised. Sometimes these thought cycles can continue for hours, and become completely overwhelming. At these times, the challenge is to get yourself out of that particular thought pattern. This isn't necessarily about changing your long-term thought patterns, but rather breaking the immediate cycle. One simple technique is a 'grounding' exercise.

A grounding exercise helps you to increase your awareness of the physical, present, world around you. Instead of thinking and worrying, focus on what is happening outside yourself. Try not to focus on concerns and scenarios in your mind, instead pay attention to details around you.

All you need to do is to follow these three steps: look, listen, feel.

- **Look**: take note of one object you can see.
- **Listen**: take note of one sound you can hear.
- **Feel**: take note of one object you can feel.

You may, for example, notice a tree outside, the noise of a truck going past, then the feel of the socks on your feet. You can repeat this process as many times as you need to, thinking of different things each time. You may even like to increase the number of items you bring your awareness to: first look for one thing you can look at, listen to and feel, then look for two things for each, then three, and so on. As you do this, your mind is focusing on the current physical world around you, and drawn away from a state of anxiety or worry. You will start to feel more relaxed, and should be able to engage more fully in tasks or activities you do once you have completed the grounding exercise.

A grounding exercise is particularly helpful if you are feeling anxious or overwhelmed, or if you simply notice that you have been caught up in your thoughts for a while and need a break. One of the great things about this exercise is that you can do it anywhere, at any time, without anyone else knowing: you could do it in the middle of a meeting, or on a date! As you practice doing grounding exercises regularly, you will find that it will become increasingly easier for your mind to refocus on present sensations.

Action 2: Mindfulness

You have probably heard of mindfulness before, but perhaps haven't quite known what it is. Or maybe you have tried it in the past but found it difficult. If this is the case, I encourage you to give it another go. 'Mindfulness' refers simply to the process of purposefully and non-judgementally paying attention to the current moment[25]. Mindfulness is another exercise that gets easier with practice, and can be an extremely helpful addition to your toolkit. Research has shown that mindfulness can help reduce stress, depression, and anxiety, as well as increasing energy levels, improving memory and concentration, and can even help with other things like sleep and pain management[26].

In a somewhat similar fashion to grounding, mindfulness helps you to take a step back from your thoughts. It allows you to observe them, rather than be consumed by them. When we experience positive and negative moments in life, our personal response and judgement of them increases their impact on us. For example, someone might experience a negative event but the way they respond might positively affect the way they ultimately feel about the situation, or alternatively someone might judge themselves harshly for an experience that was actually largely positive. Mindfulness enables you to accept your thoughts and emotions, reducing the automatic judgements that usually accompany them[24].

Begin with just two minutes of mindfulness. To start, you will need to find a comfortable position (usually sitting), somewhere you won't be interrupted, and then close your eyes. Then for two minutes, focus on your breathing: the sensation of your breath passing across your nostrils or lips, the movement of your chest and stomach, and the sounds your breath makes. Try to concentrate solely on your breathing. You can use a timer if it helps.

You will inevitably find other thoughts entering your mind during this time, and may suddenly be wondering 'has it been two minutes yet?', 'I'm starving!', 'my foot is itchy', 'this is ridiculous!', 'I feel silly', 'I need to start preparing for that meeting'. This is normal, so don't be disheartened. When you notice your mind wandering, just gently bring your attention back to your breath. Try not to be self-critical or judgemental, or try to actively push thoughts out of the way. Acknowledge the thoughts, then gently and patiently refocus on your breathing.

As well as setting aside time to specifically practice mindfulness, you may also like to incorporate some informal mindfulness as you go about your day, particularly when you are performing repetitive tasks that don't require too much active thought. During informal mindfulness, try to focus on your present actions and sensations as you do things like wash the dishes, listen to music, colour in or draw, or eat a meal. You will find that through practicing mindfulness formally, such as with the mindfulness breathing exercise, your mind will more easily enter that state in other parts of your day. Gradually this will mean that you will spend more time experiencing the present, rather than being caught up in your potentially negative thoughts.

Action 3: Gratitude

Gratitude is simply the act of deliberately focusing our mind on things we feel grateful for. Gratitude is a bit of a buzzword, and perhaps comes across sounding a little too simple to actually be of any benefit. But there is research that shows that gratitude can actually have many positive benefits. It can make people happier, improve mood, improve depressive symptoms, and make relationships more satisfying[27].

Deliberately focusing on the things you are grateful for helps to create positive neural pathways in the brain. When you do this frequently, over a prolonged period of time, you strengthen those pathways, and your brain will use them more easily. Gratitude, therefore, can be a useful tool for re-training our brains to be more positive, which helps us to live more satisfying and happy lives.

Regular gratitude exercises can be easily incorporated into your life, and you can choose an approach that suits you. You might like to practice gratitude every day, or less frequently. For example, gratitude could involve briefly paying attention to things you are grateful for each day, or focusing more intently on them at more spread out intervals. Here are some ways you could incorporate gratitude into your life:

- Each night before bed, write down three things you are grateful for.
- Once a week, for ten minutes, write in depth about one or two things you feel grateful for.
- Around the dinner table with your family, share something you are grateful for. Taking turns to share can be a great way to start a family tradition of gratitude, and share the benefits that come from showing gratitude.

- If you pray, express gratitude in your prayers.
- Communicate gratitude towards others through letters, cards, emails, or even texts.

Remember that it doesn't matter exactly what you express gratitude about - it can be profound or mundane. It can be as simple as having your basic needs met.

Don't feel that you must start lots of gratitude exercises at once. It's far better to choose one that resonates with you, and to stick to it regularly for several months, than to start lots and then feel overwhelmed and give up. We are all unique, and different strategies will work differently for each of us. If you give something a try but it's really not helping you, then either let it go and try something different, or seek some professional advice to consider modifications or support.

Burnout Story

Jack had heard about gratitude exercises previously, but doubted it would do anything. He eventually decided it was worth trying, and started making a mental list of three things he was grateful for when he brushed his teeth both in the morning and at night. He was pleasantly surprised at how this brief action shifted his mental focus. For as long as he could remember, he'd had a tendency to focus on the negatives of situations. But as he continued this gratitude exercise, he noticed a gradual shift to more often noticing the positive aspects as well.

Chapter 8
Connect

We have to remember what's important in life: friends, waffles, and work. Or waffles, friends, work. But work has to come third.
— Leslie Knope, Parks and Recreation

As people become more burnt-out, they may find that they begin to withdraw socially. This is a common symptom of burnout, and can happen for several reasons[1], such as:

- Being exhausted, and having limited energy or motivation for social engagements.
- Being emotionally drained, making it difficult to deal with the feelings and thoughts about others, which can in turn result in a loss of empathy.
- Becoming more easily irritated and frustrated, making relationships tense and less fulfilling.
- Experiencing feelings of personal inadequacy, which can lead to a loss of confidence at work, as well as at home and socially.

Strong relationships are powerful when it comes to our health. They have a positive impact on our mental health, and also our physical health[28]. When we face life's challenges, strong relationships help us to cope: we are able to process emotions better and recover more quickly. Strong relationships can also improve self-regulation[29], and help to reduce depression and anxiety. If we do suffer from depression, having strong relationships can decrease the chance of relapse following recovery. In terms of our physical health, strong relationships can reduce our risk of heart disease[30], and has been shown to contribute to longer life expectancy.

You might have many strong relationships in your life, or perhaps just a few. Or maybe you don't feel like you have any that are particularly strong at all. Keep in mind that when you are fully invested in a relationship, it won't always be wonderful, happy, and full of giggles. Humans are complex, relationships can be really tricky, and creating and sustaining a positive relationship can be hard work. Relationships also change over time, with close bonding moments, disagreements, hurt, disappointment, fun, and distance constantly moulding our friendships and connections with the people in our lives. And sometimes relationships end completely; romantic relationships end, or friendships grow apart. This can happen for a multitude of reasons, most of which don't necessarily bare any reflection on us as individuals.

Don't let challenges put you off. Friendships can bring great joy and connection. So, throw yourself in, get invested. Let yourself experience the highs of love and the joy of friendship, but also the lows of loss, hurt, disappointment, and frustration. Try not to let the fear of hurt and loss deter you from investing in relationships, but instead focus on building positive relationships. Enjoy them even if they don't last forever, or if they're difficult at times.

Burnout Story

Helen had never had loads of friends or loved big social gatherings, but had looked forward to regular catch-ups with her small group of close friends. Over recent months, though, she found herself avoiding seeing them, and making excuses for not being able to go. Her friends seemed to irritate her more than usual, and she couldn't muster the emotional energy to be supportive when they were having a hard time. When she did go, she didn't want to tell them about what she was going through, but dreaded putting on a 'happy face' and pretending everything was okay. Helen got some support with her burnout, and slowly started to see her friends again, even though it took a lot of effort to begin with. After a while, it started to feel easier again, and sometimes even enjoyable. She bravely shared with them what she had been going through, and was surprised that not only were they supportive, but that a couple of them shared that they had been through a similar experience. These friends became key parts of her support network as she continued to recover and enjoy life again.

If you want to recover from burnout, it will be a huge benefit for you to have strong relationships. You may want to strengthen your current relationships, re-establish neglected relationships, or perhaps form new ones. You don't necessarily need a plethora of friends, but the idea is to develop a small number of strong relationships which are consistent and long-standing, with frequent interaction[31]. These relationships are invaluable, providing you with people to reach out to when you feel lonely; to share exciting news with; to talk through big decisions with; to laugh with if you do something embarrassing; or to have interesting conversations with. Having strong relationships may even mean that there is someone in your life who would drop everything to help you if needed, or who would loan you a small amount of money in a difficult time. Strong relationships are about more than just what people can offer you, but also what you can share, and what you can offer them. For example they can provide you with a support network, but also bring shared joy, shared experiences, and mean that you have people in your life who you can care deeply for.

If you struggle with a mental illness such as anxiety or depression, maintaining relationships can be particularly challenging. If this is the case for you, the first thing to do is to check in with your healthcare provider, usually a GP or psychologist, and ensure that your condition is being managed adequately. Optimised treatment of the illness will give you the best starting point for forming and maintaining friendships.

Take a moment to think about your relationships. These might be friends, family, or romantic relationships. Perhaps you have lots of friends, but don't feel particularly close to any of them, or maybe you feel like you have close work friends but that the friendships are situational, just 'work friends,' and won't last beyond your current workplace. Maybe you have close friendships but you want to find ways to further strengthen these relationships, or to include new ones. Or maybe at this point in your life you don't feel like you have any close relationships at all.

Whatever your situation, there are things you can do to help find meaningful relationships or strengthen existing ones. As you read through the following ideas, consider which ones might be achievable for you in the immediate future.

Action 1: Join a community or hobby group

If you attend an activity group, such as a sporting group, a book club, a woodworking group, or a craft gathering, then there is less pressure to actively socialise all the time. Lulls in conversation are expected, and filled easily by participation in the activity itself, which often eliminates awkward silences. The fact that everyone present has an interest in that particular activity provides common ground and a starting point for connection and conversation. Even if the activity is new to you, you will at least have the shared experience of the meeting itself to draw on, and opportunities to start conversations by asking questions and learning from others.

It is advisable to make sure any group you attend is organised by someone else and not yourself, as this will enable you to cancel at the last minute if needed. If you are burnt-out you may worry that you will let people down if you don't turn up, or you may even hesitate to make plans at all for fear that your fluctuating symptoms may result in the need to cancel. If you do find yourself needing to pull out, firstly don't worry, and then if you feel comfortable, try being open about why you had to cancel. Often people will be very understanding, especially when they have an explanation rather than a mystery. Sharing your reasons could even be an opportunity to spread awareness of how you and others are affected by burnout, and potentially open up avenues of discussion in which other people feel comfortable sharing similar experiences.

Action 2: Reach out and invite

When you are burnt-out, you might find you struggle to engage in relationships. This may be particularly difficult if you are easily irritated or if you are finding it difficult to expend emotional energy on getting to know others. This in turn might make it difficult to show empathy. Perhaps you are concerned that you might not have much to offer as a friend; feeling like you are uninteresting, or not fun enough, or that people just won't like you. Or maybe you feel like people already have their own friends and there's no room for you.

So what should you do? Contact a friend or family member, and invite them to catch up. Often we wait for other people to make contact, which can lead to feelings of loneliness. In reality, other people are often waiting to be contacted too, and would actually be delighted to catch up. So, contact someone and make a plan to catch up. Spend time together, simply sharing your lives. Talk about recent events, show genuine interest in the other person, and maybe even discuss your current struggles with burnout. Opening up about your difficulties can be hard, especially if you usually take on the role of supporting others, rather than seeking advice and support for yourself. However, often sharing vulnerabilities with people you trust opens up new avenues for support and actually strengthens relationships.

You may find it helpful to prepare for a catch up by thinking of things you could share, and also things you could ask the other person about. Planning beforehand may feel a bit artificial, but if you're burnt-out, any level of social interaction can feel really difficult. Even just a small amount of thought about how you will approach a particular catch-up might give you more confidence, or help to re-establish your usual patterns of relating with others.

To build a network of strong relationships, you could try finding new ways to hang out with old friends, or explore entirely new friendships. If you don't already have a network of strong relationships, it may be helpful for you to try to expand your social network. You might like to get to know neighbours, colleagues, or people you volunteer alongside or study with. If you have kids, you could strike up conversation with other parents at a park, school, or at extracurricular activities. When you meet someone new, try not to overthink how you are coming across to them: give yourself the best chance of finding a true friend by being yourself, not being what you think others expect you to be.

If conversation feels difficult when you meet up with someone, then try finding an activity to do together; a shared experience. This could be watching a movie, helping each other with gardening, going for a walk, playing a board game, making sushi together, going to the gym, or even joining an interest group together, giving you a 'buddy' for extra comfort and confidence. Shared experiences can be a good way to build strong friendships, because rather than just catching up for coffee, sharing experiences gives you a chance to share in each other's lives more meaningfully. Also, you will then have experiences to look back on, talk about, and laugh about. Similarly to joining a hobby group, participating in an activity with someone allows you to spend time with them without being forced into long periods of conversation.

If you find that you are still struggling to interact with people, try shifting your focus to them. Show genuine interest in their lives and interests, ask questions, show that you care through listening carefully and responding with empathy. Approach relationships by thinking about how you can make the *other* person feel. If it is someone who you have recently met, try to remember their name and make sure you use it when you greet them. Look for things you can genuinely compliment them about. Listen closely to what they are saying, instead of concentrating on what you are going to say next. Ask them lots of questions about themselves. When they answer, instead of moving onto the next topic, ask for more and more detail, really trying to get to know about their lives and thoughts. You may want to bake them a cake, or take them to their favourite cafe. Surprise them with a small gift, or be there for them if they are having a difficult time. Thinking about how the other person is experiencing the friendship may help give you a new focus and nurture stronger connections.

You won't become friends with everyone you meet or organise to catch up with, but remember that this is normal. Don't worry if some friendships or relationships don't work out. You will click with some people, and not with others. Don't feel disheartened if a friendship peters out, instead learn from the experience, concentrate on the positives from that relationship, and give another friendship a go.

Maybe you are feeling distanced from a current romantic relationship, in which case the ideas explored in this chapter can be used to strengthen and nurture these intimate relationships too. Whatever the relationship, whether friendship or romantic, the important thing is to foster strong relationships by making the effort to find time to enjoy each other's company.

Chapter 9
Nourish and Move

If you consciously let your body take care of you, it will become your greatest ally and trusted partner.

— Deepak Chopra

Our bodies and minds are inseparable. What happens in our minds can affect our bodies, and the opposite is also true; how we feel in our bodies can affect our minds. Psychological factors in physical illnesses are incredibly powerful. If a patient can be made to feel cared for and secure, that alone can trigger biological changes and alter symptoms. Likewise, the way we treat our bodies can affect the way we feel, and therefore impact aspects of our mental health, including symptoms of burnout. Because of this link between our minds and bodies, burnout management must include considerations for both. Examples of the connections between our brains and our bodies can be seen every day, from the soothing effect a kiss can have on making a child's knee feel better, to the positive effect that physical exercise has on our minds. Another good example of the effect our minds can have on our bodies is demonstrated through the placebo effect, whereby it is the power of 'suggestion' on our minds, rather than a medication itself, that reduces symptoms. Physical health and mental health are so intertwined that it's impossible to really address one without the other.

The two areas we'll be looking at with regard to your physical health in this chapter are exercise and diet. For most people, these two seemingly easy components become difficult to address due to a number of reasons such as bad past experiences with attempts to improve diet or exercise levels, or layers of emotion caused by societal pressures, such as the pressure to have the perfect toned slim body, or to follow the latest fad diet. When you're burnt-out, exercising regularly and maintaining a healthy diet can become even more difficult, so when addressing these areas it is important to keep things simple.

Action 1: Regular movement

When we're overwhelmed, stressed, burnt-out, or depressed, we usually feel tired and unmotivated, so probably the last thing we feel like doing is going out and exercising! We ask ourselves 'is it really worth the effort?' The research says yes. Regular movement of our bodies has a profound effect on our mental health. It releases endorphins (the 'feel good' chemical), and also increases our levels of serotonin, which is a neurotransmitter responsible for regulating mood[7]. Together, these chemical changes in the brain help make people feel better by reducing symptoms of depression[32] and anxiety[33].

There are other emotional benefits that exercise can have, for example if you participate in an activity that involves developing or improving a skill, this in itself can result in feelings of satisfaction and accomplishment, and also build confidence in your ability to achieve things. In addition to emotional benefits, exercise has many well-documented physical health benefits, such as improved cardiovascular health, increased general fitness levels, and benefits relating to osteoporosis, type 2 diabetes, strokes, and some types of cancer[11].

Knowing that exercise is good for you is one thing, but actually doing it is often another thing entirely, particularly in the context of fatigue and loss of motivation. So, to begin with, aim to increase your level of physical activity *gradually*. Consistent and regular exercise is a fantastic goal, but if you are currently inactive then any increase is significant.

Choose an activity you think is realistically achievable. Mountain biking might not be the most appropriate activity if you live in the city, and joining a gym may not be the best option if you have to travel an hour to get to the closest one. Try to find an activity that can be worked in easily with your daily or weekly schedule. This might be walking to work, stopping at a local pool for a swim on your way home from work, weekend sports, or simply walking your dog more often. If you regularly catch up with friends, you could try going for a walk or something instead of meeting at a cafe. This could also strengthen friendships by creating shared experiences, as discussed earlier in this book. Working exercise into your normal daily life means that you won't have to specifically find time to fit exercise in; allowing you to prioritise exercise without overfilling your schedule. Whatever activity you choose initially, try to see it as an experiment to find what suits you best, rather than approaching it as a chore. Explore new activities: you may be surprised by what types of exercise you find enjoyable.

The more fun you can have, the better. Try to make 'having fun' your focus, and then exercise will happen almost as a by-product. There's no point going to the gym if it bores you to tears, or joining a dance class if you have no desire or interest in dancing. But if you love hiking, or Salsa dancing, or kayaking, or swimming, then you will find that you do these things for the joy of the activities themselves, with 'hard work' or 'exercise' far from your mind. Try to do things that leave you with a big smile on your face. It may help to think about activities you have always wanted to do but never found the time to pursue, which may even be activities you have wanted to do since you were a child. If you try something new, don't worry if you're not very good at it to start with. All skills take practice, so don't give up too easily. Enjoy the challenge and expect that it may take a few sessions to get into the swing of how it works. Finding something that is enjoyable for you will make regular exercise more sustainable long-term, and you may even find yourself looking forward to it!

So choose an activity, start slow, and don't set your expectations too high.

- Go for a walk in the bush.
- Join your neighbour when they walk the dog.
- Cycle to work.
- Go rock climbing.
- Try an adult circus class.
- Start horse riding classes.
- Go kayaking or canoeing.
- Play a team sport, either with friends, or with people you don't know as an opportunity to meet new people.
- Jog while you listen to your favourite music or an interesting podcast.
- Join a yoga class.
- Attend an adult gymnastics or acrobalance class.
- Go swimming at your local pool.
- Start your weekend with a workout at a gym.
- Learn a martial art.
- Join a dance class, such as Swing Dancing, Tango, Hip Hop, Jazz, Zumba, Salsa, Irish Dancing, or Ballet.

Work out what helps motivate you to exercise. You may find it easier to exercise if you take a friend, or participate in a group activity. Or you might find it helpful to keep some sort of record of your physical activity, such as a step-counting app, as a way to keep you motivated and track your achievements. Maybe for you, the trick is being physically active in small, frequent, 5-10 minute blocks, rather than longer sessions. Do whatever works best for you.

If you are already exercising regularly, then that's fantastic, keep it up! Be careful that you're not overdoing it. In times of stress, some people end up over-exercising, which can be problematic, particularly when it is being used as a mechanism to seek control. If this is a concern for you, your doctor will be able to guide you through a healthier approach.

Please be aware that for some people, certain types of exercise may not be appropriate, due to medical conditions or various other reasons. Plans for regular exercise may need to be carefully organised alongside a medical professional. This is especially important if you are new to exercise, pregnant, overweight, have heart disease, have major health problems, have an existing injury, or if you smoke. In these cases, it is recommended that you seek medical advice *before* commencing an exercise program.

Action 2: Good nutrition

Eating nutritious food can have a big impact on our moods and emotions[34]. A recent Australian study on depression[35] found that dietary changes can significantly reduce depressive symptoms within just three months. Poor nutrition can also have physical effects including bowel issues, fatigue, and nutrient deficiencies[11]. People experiencing burnout often find that as energy levels drop, nutrition levels also drop. This happens for many reasons, such as becoming too busy or overwhelmed to take proper meal breaks, having less motivation to prepare quality foods and therefore consuming more processed foods, or withdrawing socially from shared meal environments that used to be enjoyed.

Unfortunately, in our society, our relationship with food can often be complicated; layered with conflicting advice, judgement, personal guilt, and anxiety. Try to lay aside any negative feelings or emotions and instead start thinking positively about food and nutrition. Of course, if you have a particularly complicated history with food, this issue probably isn't something you are going to be able to solve quickly or immediately. Instead, wait until you have recovered adequately from burnout before addressing the problem. If you are suffering from a complicated food issue, I highly recommend seeing a General Practitioner, dietitian or other qualified health professional to discuss when you should begin to address this, and to help you work towards recovery.

And remember, food is about more than simple physical nutrition. It also gives us pleasure, and is part of socialising and cultural events. Food should be something fun and interesting!

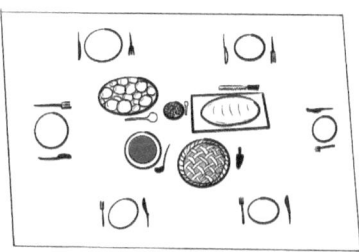

Here are five things to aim for, remembering to only do one at a time:

1. Tune-in to your body, and honour your body's feelings of hunger and satiety (i.e. fullness); eat when you're hungry, stop when you're satisfied.

2. Increase your intake of fresh fruit and vegetables. You could add a salad to your lunch, or add a few more vegetables to your evening meal.
3. Reduce your intake of processed foods. Snacking between meals is often how processed foods sneak into our diets. Consider replacing these with fresh fruit, nuts, yogurt, or veggies with a dip.
4. Give yourself permission to occasionally enjoy delicious 'treat' food, guilt-free, without labelling it as 'bad' or 'naughty'! Explore new flavours, recipes, and restaurants. When you eat, pay attention to the flavours and textures, and savour foods you love.
5. Find non-food-related coping strategies to deal with your emotions. This will be different for everyone, but could include things like going for a walk, reading, drawing, watching TV, or trying a mindfulness exercise or a relaxation technique. When you're struggling emotionally, have a read back through Chapter 4, and show yourself some compassion.

If you can gradually and consistently work towards doing these five things, you will provide yourself with a great framework for nourishing your body and mind.

Burnout Story

Sheree started off most mornings feeling pretty good. But as the day went on, she felt the pressure increasing and her workload piling up. She worried that if she took a proper break, she'd fall further behind, so she'd grab a few biscuits from the tearoom and continue working. By the end of the day, she'd be dehydrated, and desperate for a proper meal. She reluctantly followed advice to prioritise some proper breaks and nutritious meals throughout her day. Initially she struggled from anxiety throughout these breaks, worrying about all the work she wasn't getting done that would be continuing to mount. But as she got used to it, she realised that these breaks re-fuelled her, and that by taking care of herself in this way she was often actually more productive and efficient than she had been by stubbornly pushing through the day. She also felt much less depleted after work, and even had some energy left to socialise in the evening or take her dogs to the park.

Chapter 10
Values

To be yourself in a world that is constantly trying to make you something else is the greatest accomplishment.
— Ralph Waldo Emerson

Values are what help shape the way we live our lives. Having a strong sense of your values, and being aware of what gives your life meaning and purpose, will help give you clarity as you recover from burnout. Keeping your values in the forefront of your mind will help guide you in making decisions, setting priorities, keeping things in perspective, and maintaining hope for what lies ahead.

In addition to benefits for your mental health, having a strong sense of meaning in life actually leads to better physical health, too. A sense of purpose in life has been linked to reduced heart disease, better nutrition, increased fitness, reduced inflammation in our bodies, more physical reserve for when we get sick, slower cognitive decline, and even living longer[36].

Whether or not you have sat down at some point in your life and thought about your values and what gives you purpose, it's worth revisiting them now. After all, values are not the sort of thing you can 'do once then tick-off'. They evolve, change, and grow over time. They are also the type of thing that people might have a general feeling about, but have never thought about in detail. Often, instead of letting our values and purpose guide our decisions, thoughts, and actions, we tend to easily get swept up by all the little things going on in our lives; becoming consumed by our reactions to immediate events we face. We let trivial and mundane things obscure what we really care about.

You may find it interesting and insightful to do the exercises in this chapter together with a trusted friend, partner, or family member.

Action 1: Exploring your purpose

Do you have a clear idea of your core values; the things that provide meaning and purpose in your life? It's time to grab a pen and paper, and explore the deeper reasons for what you do. Set aside some time to consider the questions below, and write down your thoughts and feelings as you reflect on them. Perhaps you feel like there aren't many things at all that currently give you meaning or purpose. In this case, think about areas of your life you could explore in order to build meaning into your life. You may find that exploring the following questions will help you to form new values or discover ones that you weren't aware of. Don't worry if you struggle to answer all of them, just write down what you can.

- What motivates you?
- What makes you get out of bed in the morning?
- What gives your life purpose?
- What gives you hope?
- What gives you a sense of your place in the world?
- What roles do you fulfil that give you meaning?
- What interests and goals do you have, both large and small?
- What do you value most? Identify six things or concepts that are extremely important to you.
- What dreams and ambitions did you have as a child? As a teenager? As a young adult? What about now?
- Who do you admire? Think of people you look up to or respect; people you believe run their lives well or embody the values and core beliefs you are trying to live by.

- What would you change, or keep the same, if you had to live your life over again? Would you prioritise different things? Would you take more holidays? Would you pursue a different line of work? Would you move somewhere else? Would you spend your leisure time differently?
- If you knew you only had one year left to live, and with your remaining time and energy you could prioritise just two things, what would they be?
- Think of one or two elements of your life that are important to you, but which you are not currently managing to incorporate into your life as much as you would like to. Brainstorm some ways you could include these things in your life more frequently.
- Consider what things you commonly find annoying and frustrating, or fulfilling and joyful. Ask yourself *why* you feel that way about them. What value might it be that sits behind them? Is it a value you have identified in yourself before?

When answering these questions, be sure to include large, overarching principles as well as smaller, transient things. Larger, more long-standing principles relating to your purpose and meaning in life could be elements such as a spiritual or religious belief, a fundamental idea about your role in the world, the value you place on family, or the value of helping less fortunate people. Smaller, or more transient elements might be things like hobbies, particular jobs or roles, certain friendships, or particular personal interests. Another example of something that could add great meaning to your life but only be transient, is if you were contributing to a community event or project, which may only persist for a few days, weeks, or months.

Once you have spent some time reflecting on these questions, read back through your answers and see if there are any common themes, such as being creative, particular activities or ambitions, wanting to helping others, certain skills or work-related goals, being adventurous, strong relationships, religious values, or overcoming challenges. Try to identify the underlying values behind these things.

You might find that you write a lot in this section, or just a little.

Action 2: Defining your values

People tend to be more content and satisfied when the things they do in work and life more closely match the things they see as being important, i.e. their values. For example, if you value family but work 60 hours a week and never get to see them, you are likely to feel dissatisfied and frustrated. One study showed that the act of simply writing about the values that are important to you reduces feelings of defensiveness in general, and increases feelings of love and connection with others[37]. So, it's important to take time to think about your values, and try to live by them as much as possible.

Make a list of the five values you most identify with. Here is a list of values to get you started[38] (this is not an exhaustive list, so feel free to add any that resonate with you):

- Creativity
- Equality
- Security
- Responsibility
- Forgiveness
- Ambition

- Excitement
- Authority
- Honesty
- Respect
- Enjoying life
- Friendship
- Peace
- Justice
- Freedom
- Self-discipline
- Wisdom
- Health
- Variety in life
- Influence
- Safety
- Helping others
- Humility
- Independence
- Pleasure
- Loyalty
- Wealth
- Self-respect
- Appreciation of beauty in the world
- Curiosity
- Social recognition
- Success
- Spiritual life
- Protecting the environment
- Sense of belonging
- Privacy

If you're having difficulty deciding which values you most strongly identify with, try this exercise: Think of a time you felt happy, fulfilled or satisfied, and reflect on what was happening at that time. What do you think the factors were that contributed to that moment being particularly joyful or meaningful? Or, you may find it helpful to bring to mind someone you admire or respect, and jot down some values that they appear to encompass.

Next, rank your top five values from most important to least important. This is a crucial step, because the conflict of competing values can create tension, causing decision-making to become difficult, and contributing to a lack of fulfillment and feelings of dissatisfaction. At times when it is impossible for all our values to be met, we can refer back to our ranked list of most important values and let them guide our decisions and actions.

Action 3: Journaling

Select any value you identified in the previous exercise, and spend five minutes writing about why it is important to you. What exactly does it mean to you? Why is it important to have this value in your life? How would you define this value in relation to your life? Try to be as descriptive and specific as you can. You want to end up with a detailed and intricate description, or 'picture', of the things that bring value to your life, rather than a summary of why these values are important in general. Writing about your values in this way will help you to understand your values more deeply, and make it easier to allow these values to shape your life.

Action 4: Values in your daily life

Take some time to reflect on how you spend the hours of your life. Consider both your time spent at work (or in your primary role), as well as your 'leisure' or 'free' time. Do the things you are currently doing with your time match up to the values you have identified as being most important to you? Are there any modifications you could make to further align your daily activities with your values? Remember that to feel fulfilled in life, it is important to try to live as 'true' to your values as possible.

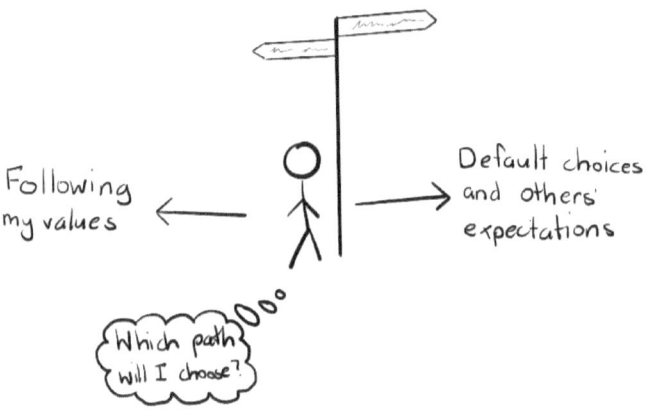

So keep your values written down in a place where you can refer back to them easily. They may help when making difficult decisions, or guide you when your life feels unfulfilling and you want to reassess your choices or consider different options.

Keep in mind that as you recover from burnout, your thought processes and decision-making abilities should improve, and your values may become clearer or even shift. Let the values you have identified in this chapter guide you on your path to recovery, but be open to change along the way.

Burnout Story

Beth felt pulled in all directions, and frequently struggled to make decisions when it felt that every option meant sacrificing something important to her. She was guided through a process of clarifying exactly what her values and priorities were, and which of these were most important. The detail and depth of clarity drastically reduced the time and mental energy she had to invest each time one of these conflicts arose. She was able to refer back to her values and much more quickly make a decision that she felt comfortable with.

What Next

The future is not some place we are going, but one we are creating. The paths are not to be found, but made. And the activity of making them changes both the maker and the destination.

— John H Schaar

Finding appropriate help

Perhaps for you, simply following the steps in this book will be enough to recover from burnout; but many people require external support or assistance. When we are burnt-out, it can be difficult to think clearly or act rationally, especially when it comes to analysing our own feelings. Because it is often very hard to navigate through burnout, it may be necessary to contact a trusted professional who has expertise in the area; someone objective who can help you find solutions and implement the best management plan for you.

So if you have decided to seek help with your recovery from burnout, it is important to find a health professional who is a good fit for you. Having a positive relationship with your health provider can have an enormous impact on your recovery, and they will also be able to review your symptoms and keep an eye out for any other underlying illnesses. When trying to find an appropriate health professional, there are several elements to look for:

- **Expertise**: someone who understands burnout and how to manage it well.
- **Trust**: someone who will maintain confidentiality, and with whom you can be open and honest.
- **Duration**: burnout recovery takes time, and it's often not 'cured', but usually requires regular measures to maintain wellbeing and prevent relapse. You do not want a health professional who 'fixes' your burnout in a couple of appointments, but rather someone who can support you through the journey for at least 3-6 months, if not more.

When considering the financial cost of getting help from a health professional, it is important to take into account the potential financial costs of leaving burnout untreated. Burnout can have devastating consequences on financial security, such as through damaged relationships, missed promotions, or ruined careers. Perhaps you have already noticed that burnout is having an effect on these areas of your life. Burnout management and recovery requires active effort, so if you feel like you need guidance or extra support, it is important to seek help. The financial cost of appointments can add up, but so can the effects of burnout. If you feel you need help desperately, you may want to steer away from free or low-cost services, such as online information, 'quick fix' blog posts, or superficial services, because they tend to be brief and provide more generic rather than personalised information.

When facing burnout, sometimes the priority needs to be finding the best care you can, as soon as you can, in order to give yourself the best chance of recovery. You will probably end up paying more for prompt services, expertise and personalised treatments, but the payoffs for receiving excellent treatment may be worth every penny. If you can't afford top quality personalised treatment, don't worry. Book an appointment with your GP and go from there. They may be able to provide some assistance in addressing the issue themselves, or recommend someone appropriate to suit your budget.

Summary

Burnout is a serious issue that often gets ignored or overlooked until it's too late, so congratulations for taking the first, hardest step of realising that you are burnt-out and admitting that you need to do something about it.

This book is a good starting point for recovery. Remember that it covers just the first ten steps to address burnout, and that there are further options available if needed. Here is a brief reminder of what this book has covered; information you have learnt and strategies to address burnout.

- Burnout can have a huge impact on your physical and mental health, but recovery is possible.
    1. Explore your current situation and dream of a better future.
    2. Reduce stress by clearing your schedule and making time for self-care.
    3. Check your health with a doctor, and schedule leave if needed.

4. Learn to show self-compassion, rather than self-criticism.
5. Set boundaries, prioritise your time, and learn to say "no".
6. Prioritise sleep and rest.
7. Learn strategies to reduce stress and manage challenges, such as grounding, mindfulness and gratitude.
8. Build strong relationships.
9. Care for your physical body, with a nourishing diet and regular exercise.
10. Live in line with your values and purpose.

- Seek external help from a qualified professional if needed.

If you have been implementing the steps in this book, you should already have noticed some benefits. If you have skimmed through quickly, that's ok, but I highly recommend going back through at a slower pace and taking time to try out some of the suggestions. With deliberate action, recovery from burnout is possible.

So, if you're burnt-out, act. Don't put it off.

You matter. Your health matters. Your life matters!

References

1. Maslach C and Leiter MP. Understanding the burnout experience: recent research and its implications for psychiatry. World Psychiatry. Jun 2016; 15(2):103-111. https://www.ncbi.nlm.nih.gov/pmc/articles/PMC4911781/ Accessed Jul 30, 2018.
2. Heinemann LV and Heinemann T. Burnout research: emergence and scientific investigation of a contested diagnosis. SAGE Open, January-March 2017: 1–12. DOI: 10.1177/2158244017697154.
http://journals.sagepub.com/doi/pdf/10.1177/2158244017697154 Accessed July 30, 2018.
3. Lifeline. Work Leading Cause of Stress. Media Release, 25th July 2014. https://www.lifeline.org.au/about-lifeline/ media-centre/media-releases/2014-articles/work-leading-cause-of-stress Accessed Apr 10, 2018.
4. Krasner MS et al. Association of an educational program in mindful communication with burnout, empathy, and attitudes among primary care physicians. JAMA. 2009; 302:1284-1293.
http://jamanetwork.com/journals/jama/fullarticle/184621 Accessed July 30, 2018.
5. Drummond D. Physician Burnout Presents Differently in Male and Female Doctors. https://www.thehappymd.

com/blog/bid/294952/Physician-Burnout-Presents-Differently-in-Male-and-Female-Doctors Accessed Jul 20, 2018.
6. Schroder HS et al. The effect of expressive writing on the error-related negativity among individuals with chronic worry. Psychophysiology, 2017; DOI: 10.1111/psyp.12990. Accessed Jul 30, 2018.
7. Suzuki W. 2015. Healthy brain, happy life: how to activate your brain and do everything better. Random House Australia Pty Ltd, New South Wales, Australia.
8. Lewinsohn P and Libet J. Pleasant events, activity schedules, and depressions. Journal of Abnormal Psychology, 1972, July, Vol 79(3):291-5.
9. Cuijpers P et al. Behavioral activation treatments of depression: A meta-analysis. Clinical Psychology Review, 2007, 27:318-326.
10. Lacovides A et al. The relationship between job stress, burnout and clinical depression. Journal of Affective Disorders, 2003, 75:209-211.
11. Murtagh J. 2011. Murtagh's General Practice, fifth edition. McGraw-Hill Australia Pty Ltd, New South Wales, Australia.
12. Black Dog Institute. Clinical Resources. https://www.blackdoginstitute.org.au/clinical-resources. Accessed June 10, 2018.
13. Germer CK. 2009. The Mindful Path To Self-Compassion: freeing yourself from destructive thoughts and emotions. The Guildford Press, New York, USA.
14. Neff K. 2011. Self-Compassion: The Proven Power Of Being Kind To Yourself. Harper Collins, New York, USA.
15. Australian Psychological Society. Stress. https://www.psychology.org.au/for-the-public/Psychology-topics/Stress Accessed Sep 16, 2018.

16. Neff K and Germer C. 2018. The Mindful Self-Compassion Workbook: A Proven Way to Accept Yourself, Build Inner Strength, and Thrive. The Guilford Press, New York, USA.
17. Kossek EE and Ozeki C. Work-family conflict, policies, and the job-life satisfaction relationship: a review and directions for organizational behavior-human resources research. Journal of Applied Psychology, Apr 1998, 83(2):139-149.
18. Allen TD et al. Consequences associated with work-to-family conflict: a review and agenda for future research. Journal of Occupational Health Psychology, 2000, 5(2):278-308.
19. Sommers-Flanagan R et al. Exploring the edges: boundaries and breaks. Ethics and behavior, 1998, 8(1):37-48.
20. Ramar K and Olson E. Management of common sleep disorders. American Family Physician, 2013, Aug 15, 88(4):231-238.
21. Clarke D et al. Beyondblue guide to the management of depression in primary care: a guide for health professionals. http://resources.beyondblue.org.au/prism/file?token=BL/0484. Accessed Oct 18, 2018.
22. Boyce P and Barriball E. Circadian rhythms and depression. Australian Family Physician, May 2010, 39(5):307-310.
23. Keng SL et al. Effects of mindfulness on psychological health: a review of empirical studies. Clinical Psychological review, Aug 2011, 31(6):1041-1056.
24. Hassed C et al. Enhancing the health of medical students: outcomes of an integrated mindfulness and lifestyle program. Advanced Health Sciences Education Theory and Practice, 2009, 14(3):387-398.

25. Kabat-Zinn J. Mindfulness-based interventions in context: past, present, and future. Clinical Psychology: Science and Practice, 2003, 10(2):144-156.
26. Wolkin JR. Cultivating multiple aspects of attention through mindfulness meditation accounts for psychological well-being through deceased rumination. Psychology Research and Behavior Management, Jun 2015, 8:171-180.
27. Wood AM et al. Gratitude and well-being: A review and theoretical integration, Clinical Psychology Review (2010), doi:10.1016/j.cpr.2010.03.005.
28. Umberson D and Montez JK. Social relationships and health: a flashpoint for health policy. Journal of Health and Social Behavior, 2010, 51(S):S54-S66.
29. Seeman TE. Health promoting effects of friends and family on health outcomes in older adults. American Journal of Health Promotion, 2000, 14(6):362–370.
30. Orth-Gomer K et al. Lack of social support and incidence of coronary heart disease in middle aged Swedish men. Psychosomatic Medicine, 1993, 55:37-43.
31. Baumeister RF and Leary MR. The need to belong: desire for interpersonal attachments as a fundamental human motivation. Psychological Bulletin, 1995, 117(3):497-529.
32. Cooney GM et al. Exercise for depression. Cochrane Database of Systematic Reviews 2013, Issue 9.
33. Stathopoulous G et al. Exercise interventions for mental health: a quantitative and qualitative review. Clinical Psychology: Science and Practice. 2006, 13: 179-193.
34. O'Neil A et al. Relationship between diet and mental health in children and adolescents: a systematic review. American Journal of Public Health, 2014, 104(10):e31-e42.
35. Jacka FN et al. A randomised controlled trial of dietary improvement for adults with major depression: the SMILES trial. BMC Medicine, 2017(15):23.

36. Gregorevic K. The power of purpose. Oct 28, 2017. https://drkategregorevic.com/the-power-of-purpose/#gs.70f445.
37. Crocker J et al. Why does writing about important values reduce defensiveness? Self-affirmation and the role of positive other-directed feelings. Psychological Science, Jul 2008; 19(7):740-7.
38. Schwartz, S. 2012. An overview of the Schwartz theory of basic values. Online Readings in Psychology and Culture, 2(1).

About the author

Dr Amy Imms is a medical doctor, author, and public speaker, who helps people struggling with or at risk of burnout. As a former General Practitioner, Amy has seen countless cases of burnout amongst both patients and colleagues, and was troubled by how late people tended to seek help, increasing the severity of symptoms, and recovery time. Amy's personal experience of burnout as she juggles five young children and a career has added a further dimension to her understanding of the condition and methods for managing it.

Amy is on a mission to raise awareness of burnout as a huge problem facing our society, to reduce stigma, guide workplaces in preventing burnout, and assist individuals in their recovery. Amy strives to focus not just on providing information, but making it practicable within normal, full, complicated lives. This has required considered adaptation of the basic principles of burnout prevention and recovery to suit audiences, including parents, professionals, small business owners, healthcare workers, crafting groups, community leaders, managers, and carers of children with special needs.

One of her favourite audiences to teach is children, using fun activities and creative exercises to help our next generation of adults to expand self-awareness and learn how to care for their minds.

Amy has founded The Burnout Project so that anyone who is concerned about someone being burnt-out can anonymously nominate them to receive a copy of this book along with other items.

Workshops and Services

Dr Amy Imms provides a range of services which may be of assistance to you or your workplace:

- Group burnout recovery programs
- Children's workshops
- Creativity and wellbeing workshops and events
- Training for workplace representatives to learn how to prevent and manage burnout and facilitate education and awareness within their workplace
- Workplace burnout workshops and talks
- Speaking at conferences and events
- Individual burnout counselling

Find out more about which options may be best for your situation at DrAmyImms.com/services

The Burnout Project

If you are concerned that a friend, family member or colleague is burnt-out and you're looking for something you can do to help them, then you may like to send them a Burnout Package.

Recharge Packages contain a copy of this book along with a notebook, pen and reminder card. Nourish Boxes include additional items to encourage self-care, such as a journal, gift cards, loose leaf tea, handmade soap, and a printed workbook.

The Burnout Project is designed to help individuals to acknowledge or recognise that they are burnt out, and prompt them to act and seek assistance. It is designed to show them that there is something that they can do about burnout, and give them hope. It will show that someone else has noticed their struggle, and cared enough to do something to help them.

If you would like to purchase a bulk quantity of this book or Burnout Packages for your workplace, organisation or event, please email info@theburnoutproject.com.au

Find out more about The Burnout Project, and the specific packages currently available at theburnoutproject.com.au

www.ingramcontent.com/pod-product-compliance
Lightning Source LLC
Chambersburg PA
CBHW032043290426
44110CB00012B/935